THE DARKER FACE OF THE EARTH

WORKS BY RITA DOVE

POETRY

Selected Poems
Pantheon / Vintage, 1993

Grace Notes
W.W. Norton, 1989

Thomas and Beulah
Carnegie-Mellon, 1986

Museum
Carnegie-Mellon, 1983

The Yellow House on the Corner
Carnegie-Mellon, 1980

FICTION

Through the Ivory Gate, a novel
Pantheon, 1992

Fifth Sunday, short stories
Callaloo Fiction Series,
University of Kentucky, 1985

DRAMA

The Darker Face of the Earth
Story Line Press, 1994

"The Siberian Village", a one-act play
(in *Callaloo*, Vol. 14/2, 1991)

THE DARKER FACE
OF THE EARTH

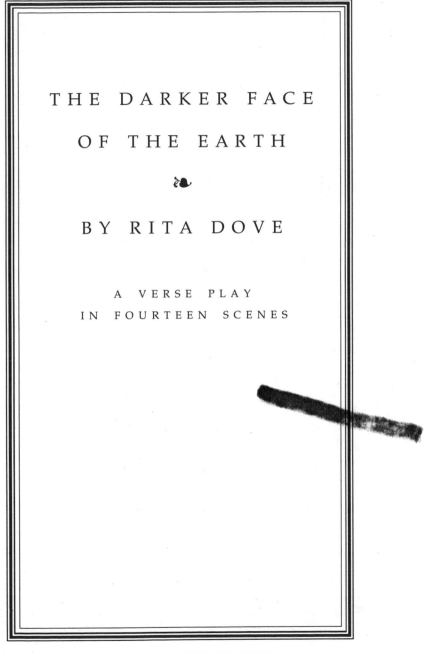

BY RITA DOVE

A VERSE PLAY
IN FOURTEEN SCENES

STORY LINE PRESS
1994

All performance rights are with the author. For performance permission, contact in writing: Rita Dove, Department of English, Wilson Hall, University of Virginia, Charlottesville, VA, 22903.

Published by Story Line Press, Inc., Three Oaks Farm, Brownsville, OR 97327

This publication was made possible thanks in part to the generous support of the Nicholas Roerich Museum, the Andrew W. Mellon Foundation, the National Endowment for the Arts, and our individual contributors.

The author wishes to thank her husband, Fred Viebahn, for his encouragement and help.

Library of Congress Cataloging-in-Publication Data

Dove, Rita.
        The darker face of the earth : a verse play in fourteen scenes / by Rita Dove.
        p.   cm.
        ISBN 0-934257-74-4 : $10.95
        1. South Carolina—History—1775–1865—Drama. 2. Women plantation owners—South Carolina—Drama. 3. Mothers and sons—South Carolina—Drama. 4. Afro-Americans—South Carolina—Drama. 5. Slaves—South Carolina—Drama.   I. Title.
PS3554.0884D68   1994
812'.54—dc20   93-39433
                                                CIP

For my daughter,

Aviva Chantal Tamu Dove-Viebahn

C A S T

Female slaves:
  PHEBE
  PSYCHE, also called "Sack"
  OLD SLAVE WOMAN
  SCYLLA
  ROSE, the midwife
  DIANA, a child
  OLD PRAYER WOMAN
  TICEY, Amalia's personal servant

Male slaves:
  ALEXANDER
  MALE SLAVE
  SCIPIO
  AUGUSTUS NEWCASTLE
  HECTOR

The whites:
  AMALIA JENNINGS
  LOUIS, Amalia's husband
  DOCTOR
  JONES, the overseer

The black conspirators:
  NED
  LEADER
  BENJAMIN SKEENE
  HENRY BLAKE

Other slaves and conspirators

Some characters can be played by the same actor—
for example, Doctor/Jones, Rose/Ticey, Psyche/Diana.

STAGE

The set consists of various levels. Scene changes are indicated by light-ing. Bleachers have been erected downstage right and left; these are for the SLAVES, who function as a chorus. They are onstage throughout the play—when not acting, they take their places on the benches as spectators.

The action takes place in antebellum South Carolina.

In order to facilitate reading of the script, slave speech has been mostly standardized.

FIRST SCENE

(PHEBE, a slave girl in her early teens, runs onstage. Skinny and electric, she is chuckling to herself as she enters.)

PHEBE	What some people won't do for attention! Sure, he's alright-looking — but that ain't qualification enough for the big white bed in the big white house! *(laughs at her own wit)*
PSYCHE	*(offstage)* Phebe! Phebe! You up there?
PHEBE	Here I am, Sack! *(PSYCHE enters. She is petite, shy; though not much older than PHEBE, she treats her like a little sister.)*
PSYCHE	You shouldn't go running off by yourself, child. No telling what might happen.
PHEBE	What can happen? All the white folks are inside.

PHEBE (con't.)	*(giggles, points)*
	Look: Hector on the porch.
PSYCHE	Leave him be, poor soul.
PHEBE	Anybody crazy enough to think what he thinks —
PSYCHE	Shush now, chile! I don't want to hear it.
	(PHEBE shrugs. The other slaves begin to straggle in.)
PHEBE	What took you all so long? Slower than a pack of lame turtles.
ALEXANDER	*(a dignified man in his fifties)*
	"Us all" 'tain't quite so spry as you, gal. Nor as eager — The way you been carrying on a body'd think it was your child being born up there in the big house!
PSYCHE	Alexander, you gotta admit ain't been nothing more exciting around here since Massa Louis fell off that new race horse last spring!

PHEBE	Shh!
	(Everyone freezes.)
	I thought I heard something.
PSYCHE	Aw, girl —
OLD SLAVE WOMAN	Rose will send word soon as it's over. Must be a hard birthin'.
SCYLLA	*(a tall dark woman in her thirties)*
	You know what they say about a hard birth: nothing but trouble ever after.
OLD SLAVE WOMAN	No: "Hard birth, the trouble worth." He'll be a joy to his mother to the end of her life.
MALE SLAVE	Another little massa around the place. I hope he dies.
PHEBE	It might be a girl.
PSYCHE	You better wish it ain't.

SCYLLA

Nothing but trouble, I tell you.
Nothing but trouble.

(During this exchange the slaves take their places on the benches. The lights come up on AMALIA's bedroom. AMALIA JENNINGS lies in a canopy bed, a thickly-swaddled babe in her arms. She is an attractive young white woman who exhibits more intelligence and backbone than is generally credited to a southern belle.)

(The DOCTOR, a middle-aged whiskered gentleman, is pacing the floor. AMALIA appears amused.)

AMALIA

Well, Doctor, isn't he beautiful?

DOCTOR

My God, Amalia — why didn't
you tell me? We could have done
something. There are ways.
And why did you call
that nigger midwife in here?

AMALIA

I thought you might need
help. And if you keep on
pacing the floor, "that nigger midwife"
will think you're doing some
primitive fertility dance!

DOCTOR

This is serious, Amalia. Lord knows
I watched your father try

to bring you up a proper lady.
He doted on you — I suppose
you never forgave him for that.

AMALIA

Don't get melodramatic, doctor.
You'll frighten my son.

(baby raises a cry)

AMALIA

See!

(Among the slaves, SCYLLA stands up and grabs her stomach.)

SCYLLA

Oh! Oh!

OTHERS

What is it, Scylla?
What is it?

SCYLLA

It's born. It's out
in the world.

(The slaves look at her in fear.)

ALEXANDER

Lord have mercy.

(AMALIA's husband LOUIS rushes into the bedroom. LOUIS is a handsome, if rather weak-spined, man in his thirties. The DOCTOR holds LOUIS back while trying to prevent ROSE the midwife from peeking in.)

LOUIS

Doctor —

DOCTOR	Everything's fine. Just go on back outside and I'll let you know.
	(LOUIS tears himself from the DOCTOR's grasp and rushes over to his wife. The DOCTOR blocks ROSE, who is just about to step into the room.)
DOCTOR	What are you standing there gawking for? Get out!
	(shoves her out, then grabs her arm)
	Don't leave this hall, you hear me? Don't make a move or say a word to anyone until I tell you so.
	(ROSE exits slowly.)
AMALIA	What, Louis — struck dumb? And after such a show of devotion! Isn't he a fine strapping boy?
LOUIS	You bitch!
AMALIA	So you can stroll out by the cabins any fine night you please, but if I summon a buck up to the house, I'm a bitch?

14

(laughs)

Well then, I'm a bitch.

(looking at the baby)

He certainly is pretty.
No wonder
they have so many of them.

DOCTOR

This is unnatural.

LOUIS

Who is it? I'll have him whipped to shreds
for raping —

AMALIA

It wasn't rape, and you know it.
He brought iced lemon water
up to my room and left
half an hour later.
Every day you saw him —
but did you ever say one word?

AMALIA

(to the DOCTOR)

Daddy knew he was weak.
He tried to keep me from
marrying him, but I was in love
with riding boots and the smell
of shaving cream and bourbon.
I was in love with a cavalry man
and nothing could stop me,
not even Daddy!

AMALIA (con't.)	*(to LOUIS)*
	But not even Daddy suspected
	where you would seek your satisfaction.
	As long as you let a slave man
	bring your wife iced drinks
	instead of doing it yourself,
	as long as a black man crawled over
	the perfumed limbs of your wife,
	you thought you had all
	the freedom in the world —
	it was your right
	to pull on those riding boots
	and stalk little slave girls.
	You enjoy their fear,
	don't you? God knows
	what you do to them in
	the name of ownership.
	And now, dear Louis,
	in the name of ownership
	you will not harm this child
	or the father of this child.
LOUIS	Then I swear I'll kill you —
	(lunges toward her, the DOCTOR restrains him)
DOCTOR	Calm yourself. They might hear.
LOUIS	Get rid of that bastard!
DOCTOR	You're upset.

LOUIS	*(frenzied whisper)*
	You can do it! Do it! Do it! An injection of morphine, and no one will be the wiser!
AMALIA	Why are you whispering, gentlemen? I tell you, no harm shall come to this child.
DOCTOR	*(motioning to LOUIS to let him handle it)*
	Now Amalia, you can't be serious. How will you ever manage to keep your slaves under control once they know you bore a black child? And the neighbors! There'll be no credit at any store in Charleston. It's suicide. Is this baby worth destroying your entire life?
AMALIA	Who said I wanted to keep him?
DOCTOR	Then you agree —
AMALIA	I don't agree to murder. After all, this child is valuable property.
DOCTOR	You would sell your own child?
AMALIA	And you would kill it?

17

DOCTOR	All right, all right.
	I have a friend in Charleston
	who likes raising slaves
	from the ground up.
	I'll talk to him. But listen
	to me, Amalia, and listen good.
	I won't tell him
	where I got this baby. Instead
	I'll sing the story of the distraught wife
	who refused to be confronted
	daily with the evidence of a husband's
	wandering lust. Everyone must think
	the baby's father is the one
	who's white.
	(LOUIS starts to protest.)
	You can have as many
	little black bastards as you please —
	no one will fault you.
	Let it be.
LOUIS	What about the niggers? They're out
	on the lawn, waiting for news.
DOCTOR	We'll say the baby expired
	directly after birth, took one breath
	and died. And that I've taken it away.
LOUIS	No funeral? Niggers love funerals.
DOCTOR	Too risky. No —

18

Amalia didn't want a funeral.
They'll believe it. They have no choice.

(to AMALIA)

You better make sure the father
keeps his mouth shut.
If you know who he is.

AMALIA

(mock indignation)

Doctor, I happen to be a very
particular woman.

(in an amused tone)

He won't talk.
And if he did, who would believe him?
I must say, Doctor,
your ingenuity surprises me.
It's what I would call a
master plan. Now —
you two gentlemen, please:
go spread the sad tidings.
I'll get the child ready.

(DOCTOR and LOUIS leave. AMALIA carefully wraps the baby and then reaches for the
round, white wicker sewing basket trimmed with
red velvet rosettes next to her bed. She emp-
ties the basket and puts the baby into it. Before closing the lid she looks inside tenderly.)

19

AMALIA	Well, little darky, guess I saved your life.
	(The lights come up on DOCTOR, LOUIS, and ROSE.)
ROSE	How's Miss Jennings, suh? The baby sure sounds like a big one!
DOCTOR	The baby's dead.
ROSE	Dead? But I heard it cry!
DOCTOR	He cried out once. Poor little thing had no more breath left.
ROSE	Now if that ain't the strangest thing…
LOUIS	*(sharply)* What's so strange about it? The baby just up and died. Happens all the time.
DOCTOR	Your mistress in there crying her eyes out with grief, and you… look at you, standing here arguing! Now go on! Go on out to those niggers — I know you got them waiting by the porch. Tell them there'll be no wailing and moaning, no singing, no mighty sorry ma'am.

Miss Jennings wants no funeral.
Miss Jennings wants to forget.
Go on now, scat!

(ROSE exits.)

Let's get this over with.

LOUIS   Go ahead. I — I'll wait here.

(The DOCTOR looks hard at LOUIS, then goes in to AMALIA.)

DOCTOR   Ready? Well, well. I'll say
one thing for you, Amalia Jennings —
you are your father's daughter.

(He exits with the basket. AMALIA turns to the side and buries her face in the pillows.)

LOUIS   Got him?

(laughs)

This is one Moses
won't see the promised land!

DOCTOR   What would you have me do?
Amalia has forbidden it.

LOUIS   Amalia! She's got no rights to him.
You just make sure
we never set eyes on him again.

LOUIS (con't.)	That's the only way.
	(DOCTOR remains silent)
	What's the matter? Aren't you a man?
DOCTOR	Even though this isn't the way the world was meant to be, I have never killed a child I've brought into this world.
	(thinking hard)
	Listen — I promised Amalia I'd take the baby to Charleston to be sold. And I will do so. But it's a long ride into town.
LOUIS	What do you mean?
DOCTOR	Anything could happen on the way...
LOUIS	I knew you'd come through!
DOCTOR	Not by my own hand! I will not be responsible! But if, without my knowledge, something should have found its way into that basket — some sharp object I know nothing about — well, then, on the way to Charleston... I would not be responsible.

LOUIS	I see. I see. Wait —
	(exits, returning immediately with a pair of spurs)
	You have a hard ride ahead of you, Doctor. These spurs might come in handy.
DOCTOR	Thank you. Just put them with my things.
	(turns his back while LOUIS puts the spurs in the sewing basket)
LOUIS	Have a pleasant journey.
DOCTOR	I will try.
	(starts to leave, turns)
	But Louis — should the child still be breathing when I arrive, I'll go ahead as planned, understood? I will not harm him with my own hands!
	(exits)
	(Blackout.)

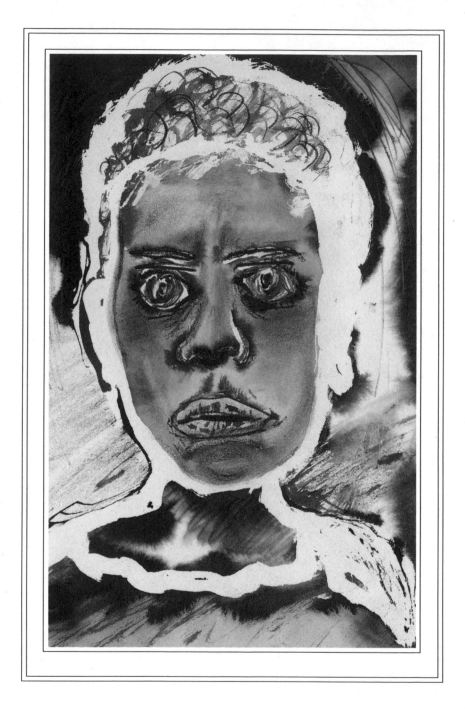

SECOND SCENE

(Twenty years later. The slaves hum a song as they go about the motions of cotton picking. JONES, the white overseer, walks back and forth. As he exits, one young slave, DIANA, sinks to the ground.)

ALEXANDER	Move it gal, or you'll feel it later!
PHEBE	*(helping her up)* Lift in your knees. Try not to think about your blood. Tomorrow you can rest.
DIANA	*(derisively)* Blessed is the Sabbath!
PHEBE	Better get used to it; you'll have to survive it every month. *(AMALIA enters, in riding clothes and with her whip in hand.)*
AMALIA	What's this?
PHEBE	How de do, ma'am. Diana don't feel well —
AMALIA	You aren't here to play doctor, Phebe. She seems healthy to me — young and fresh, good stock.

AMALIA (con't.) (*looks with disgust*)

Lazy, stinking pack!
No wonder this place is going
to wrack and ruin; I swear
I've seen cows smarter than you!
Don't stand there staring at
your ugly feet — get back to work
or your backs will tell the story.
Jones!

JONES (*rushing in*)

Yes, Miss Jennings?

AMALIA I'll see you this evening
up at the house.

(*strides off*)

JONES (*mops his forehead with a huge handkerchief, cracks his whip*)

Get to work!

(*exits*)

PHEBE She gets eviler by the hour.

ALEXANDER Ain't right, a woman
running the plantation like that.

MALE SLAVE Woman? She's more man than woman.

PHEBE	And more devil than man.
ALEXANDER	Ever since she lost that child.
PHEBE	Go on now, Alexander — you and your soft-headed notions.
ALEXANDER	'Tain't soft-headed at all. It's just that white folks feel a loss as much as we do, 'cept they ain't used to losing. I tell you, the day she lost that baby boy Miss Amalia went crazy in the head.
PHEBE	That's not what old Rose used to say.
DIANA	Who's Rose?
PHEBE	Used to be midwife here. Died before you were born. I never knew her as anything but an old woman; why, she even helped your mama into the world. Old Rose was at the house the night Miss Amalia went into labor.
DIANA	Tell me 'bout my mama again, Phebe.
PHEBE	Psyche? She was the sister I never had. She was... strong, but gentle. You were just a few days old when she died. Childbirth can kill the strongest woman.

ALEXANDER	Or kill the child.
SCYLLA	*(Twenty years have changed her considerably. She is severely bent over and walks with a limp. There is something fearful in her gaze.)*
	You still believe the white folks? That baby weren't born dead. Rose heard it cry. Doctor claimed it died and I seed him carry it off in a basket, but it weren't dead. I felt it kick.
DIANA	You felt the baby —
PHEBE	Scylla's got powers.
ALEXANDER	Conjure-powers.
SCYLLA	Before that night I was just like any other slave, didn't know my foot from a mule's. There was a veil afore my eyes. If it weren't for that baby I'd still be seeing nothing but dirt and the backside of a mule.
ALEXANDER	Scylla got her powers that night.
SCYLLA	*(staring at DIANA who shrinks back)*
	The child was born alive. Where I stood I felt the power churn in me and the veil

snatched from my eyes;
then over the hill
I saw bad times a-coming.
Bad times a-coming over the hill
on mighty horses. Horses snorting
as they galloped through slave cabin
and pillared mansion alike,
horses whinnying as they trampled
black and white folks alike.
Like a thin black net
the curse settled over the land.
The curse touched four people:
black woman, black man,
white woman, white man.
When the curse came over the hill
I stood up to meet it.
It entered me, and I fell
to the ground. My womb
dried up. I couldn't speak
for three days. But the power was in me,
and I held the curse back.

DIANA   Who were they?
                 Who were the four people?

SCYLLA   Black woman, black man,
                 white woman, white man.
                 Hector was a slave in the fields
                 until Miss Amalia took him up
                 to the big house. He followed her around
                 like her own right shoe:
                 when she fell sick

29

SCYLLA (con't.)   he brought her iced lemon water;
                    when she started to show,
                    he helped her down the stairs;
                    when the baby kicked, he soothed her.
                    But when her time came
                    he had to sit out by the porch
                    like the rest of us, and when
                    Rose brought the news
                    Hector fell to his knees
                    and ate dirt like a worm.
                    Now he lives alone
                    in a shack in the swamp
                    and catches snakes by the river.
                    Black woman, black man — both twisted
                    when the curse came over the hill.
                    But where the slave turned to grief,
                    the master turned to business.
                    Miss Amalia picked up a whip
                    and hiked up her skirts
                    to pull on man's boots.
                    But Massa Louis... Massa Louis
                    stopped coming to the quarters at night.
                    He pulled off his riding boots
                    and shut himself in the upstairs study.
                    From time to time he'd call his manservant
                    to summon up a wench, but
                    that stopped a whiles back —

                    (with a significant look at DIANA)

                    just about when you came along.
                    Some nights you can see him
                    in his dressing gown, staring at the sky.

They say he has machines
that can measure the stars.

(whispers as if telling a secret)

Black woman, black man;
white woman, white man:
four people were touched by the curse,
but the curse is still not complete.

DIANA

I'm scared.

PHEBE

(in spite of herself)

Did you have to tell her everything, Scylla?
She's just a child.

SCYLLA

She's old enough to know.
And you should know better.

(to PHEBE directly)

Why don't you come visit me
tomorrow evening, Phebe —
after the moon's set?

PHEBE

(frightened)

Aw, Scylla —

SCYLLA

It'll be pitch dark. Take care
you don't trip on the way.

THIRD SCENE

(The big house. AMALIA is looking through some papers as JONES enters.)

JONES	Yes, Miss Jennings?
AMALIA	*(without looking up)*
	Sit down.
JONES	Sorry about that incident this afternoon, ma'am. I didn't think it would do no harm if someone took some care of that little gal.
	(almost helplessly)
	The little gal seemed real sick, you know, ma'am.
AMALIA	Mr. Jones, I'm well aware you come fresh from the well-groomed slave holdings of Dawson's Plantation. And I was not so naive, upon hiring you, to believe that none of Dawson's high-minded economic philosophy had rubbed off on you. Here, however, we give slaves what they deserve, and this bunch deserves no better than what I give them. But that's not what I called you for. I bought a new buck yesterday: here are his papers.

JONES	*(glancing through the documents)*
	Miss Jennings! You can't be serious!
AMALIA	Something wrong, Jones?
JONES	*(reading)*
	"Augustus Newcastle, age 20, formerly of Captain Henry Newcastle..." Ma'am, that slave's the most talked-about nigger along the southern seaboard!
AMALIA	Good! We'll be famous.
JONES	Ma'am?
AMALIA	After we show them all how to manage a slave!
JONES	*(lost in thought)*
	Story goes he belonged to an English sea captain who treated him like his own son, even promised him his freedom in his will. But the brother who took over the execution of the estate thought better of it and sold the boy. After that, the nigger went wild — they lost count of how many times he ran off, how many times they caught him...
	(leafs through papers frantically)

Here it is: "Twenty-two
separate acts of aggression and rebellion."
Twenty-two separate acts!

AMALIA

That's why I got him so cheaply.

JONES

But Miss Jennings, twenty-two! They say
his back's so laced with scars
it's as rutted as a country road. Rumor has it
he knows how to read and write. If you don't
    mind
my saying so, ma'am, an educated nigger
brings nothing but trouble. As sure as
I'm standing here, he'll stir up the others.

AMALIA

(to herself)

I wonder how smart he is.

JONES

It's a wonder no one ever killed him.

AMALIA

(looking off)

My daddy was the best plantation owner
in these parts. He could tell
when a nigger was playing sick
or had soaked the rice to fill up a quota.
This household hummed like a ship.
I was his apprentice: he taught me everything
and signed this whole plantation
over to me before he died.
Not to Louis — to me.
Over twenty years I've run this place

AMALIA (con't.)	and never met a nigger I couldn't handle.
	(her tone sharpens)
	I own Augustus Newcastle, and I'll make him serve up. Any more objections?
JONES	No, ma'am. Sorry, ma'am.
AMALIA	They're bringing him over tonight. Put him in the barn and chain him down; you can show him around tomorrow. Then we'll decide the best place for him. If he's as smart as they say he might be able to oversee the ginning. You may go.
	(JONES looks at her for a moment, then exits. AMALIA remains sitting, bent over the accounting books.)
	(Blackout.)

FOURTH SCENE

(Sunday. The slaves have been "let out in the fields" to occupy themselves as they please. They gradually divide into two groups — the
PLAYERS and the PRAYERS. The PLAYERS joke, tell stories, and
dance. The PRAYERS are quieter; and though a "shout" will be held
that evening, they are already chanting and praying. As the lights go
up, the groups are rivaling each other in melody, the PRAYERS hum-
ming in minor key while the PLAYERS counterpoint with a jauntier
tune. SCIPIO enters, excited. He is in his twenties, a happy-go-lucky,
playboy type. He sits down with the PLAYERS.)

SCIPIO	Have you seen the new man? Mister Jones been showing him around.
PHEBE	I saw 'em down by the gin house. That's one wild nigger.
ALEXANDER	He spent last night chained in the barn. Chained!
PHEBE	He's that runaway, you know — that bright-skinned nigger they say's run off so many times no one keep count anymore!
DIANA	And nobody ever tried to kill him?

SCIPIO

(shrugs)

Must be mighty tough.

(significantly)

Heard tell he's sailed the seas!

DIANA

Did he sail the seas to Canada?

(Shocked silence. Even the PRAYERS stop praying and look at her.)

ALEXANDER

Gal, don't let nobody hear you
say that word — and I mean nobody.
Miss Amalia'll have your head
on a plate. You ain't supposed
to know nothing 'bout... that place.
As far as you concerned there's nothing in
    this world
but South Carolina and this here plantation.

(AUGUSTUS enters, followed by a watchful JONES. AUGUSTUS is a tall, powerfully built man with caramel-toned skin and piercing yellow-ringed eyes. His righteous anger is thinly concealed behind his slave mannerisms. There is defiance in every "Massa" he utters. JONES tries to bluff his way with a squeaky bravado.)

JONES

Here's the new nigger you all
been whispering about!

(to AUGUSTUS)

You're lucky you got here on a Sunday.
Tomorrow you'll get a taste
of how things run around here.
First horn at day-clean!

(*JONES exits. There is a moment's awkward silence as AUGUSTUS calmly surveys the two groups. Then he smiles.*)

SCIPIO

Welcome, stranger, welcome.
Come rest your heels.

(*AUGUSTUS slowly sits down.*)

What's your name, stranger?

AUGUSTUS

Augustus.

SCIPIO

Au-gus-tus? Ain't never heard
that one before. What kind of name is that?

AUGUSTUS

The name of a king.

(*Uneasy silence. In an attempt to smooth things over, PHEBE leans towards AUGUSTUS confidentially.*)

PHEBE

Don't pay Scipio no mind.
He's always making jokes.
I'm Phebe. And this little girl
was born and raised
on this here plantation.

(*pushes DIANA, who is hovering close to PHEBE, over to AUGUSTUS*)

AUGUSTUS	What's your name, child?
DIANA	(shyly)
	Diana.
AUGUSTUS	My, my. The sun and the moon all in one morning!
	(The slaves look bewildered. He laughs kindly.)
	Don't mind me. I'm just proud to meet you all.
	(looking over to the PRAYERS)
	Proud, do you hear? You are good people.
OLD PRAYER WOMAN	Amen!
	(The PRAYERS take up their chant again. AUGUSTUS rises, walks upstage and stands looking into the distance. The PLAYERS decide to let him be, although they are curious. Only DIANA, fascinated, keeps staring at him.)
PHEBE	Come on, Scipio, give us a story.
SCIPIO	You always wanting a story! How many stories you think I got? You think I was born with them?

PHEBE	I think you grow them in your sleep. Go on, now.
SCIPIO	Well, I ain't got a story this time.
PLAYERS	Aw, Scipio! You dog!
SCIPIO	But I got a song:

(accompanies himself on the banjo)

The possum said, don't hurt me,
I'm harmless if you please!
The nigger said, I'm harmless, too,
And got down on his knees.

The possum cocked his little head
And contemplated long;
You're running just like me, he said
And joined into the song.

Old Mr. Coon just happened by
Where the two sang merrily;
I don't trust you, cried Mr. Coon,
Why, you just as black as me!

(Laughter. DIANA walks over to AUGUSTUS.)

DIANA	What you looking at?
AUGUSTUS	Just looking.
DIANA	Ain't nothing out there but the swamp.

AUGUSTUS	Do you know what's beyond that swamp?
DIANA	What?
AUGUSTUS	The world.
PHEBE	*(to SCIPIO)*
	Is that all?
SCIPIO	No, there's more.
	(sings)

You're just as black as me, Coon said,
But your tail ain't quite so long!
Then Mr. Coon ran in the woods
And wouldn't join their song.

The nigger wrapped his fingers
Around the possum's throat.
The possum didn't have the time
to sing another note.

That night the nigger had himself
A pot of possum stew.
That harmless meat is just the thing
To warm your innards through!

DIANA	What did you mean by the sun and the moon?
AUGUSTUS	What?

DIANA

The sun and the moon.
You asked my name and then you said
you had the sun and the moon all in one day.

AUGUSTUS

You're a curious one, aren't you?
Well, I'll tell you: a long time ago
there were people who believed
there were gods to look after the earth and
    the sky.
Phoebus was the god of the sun.
Your friend's name is Phebe,
which stands for the sun. And your name
stands for the moon, because
Diana was the name of the Moon goddess.
People wrote poems to Diana,
Goddess of the Moon.

DIANA

What's poems?

AUGUSTUS

A poem is...

(looking over at SCIPIO)

...like a song without music.

(looks off towards the swamp)

Who's that old man?

DIANA

(runs back to PHEBE)

Phebe! Hector's
coming up from the swamp!
He scares me!

PHEBE	Don't worry. He talks kind of crazy sometimes, but he don't hurt nobody.
	(to AUGUSTUS)
	You know a lot.
AUGUSTUS	Nothing you couldn't learn if you had the chance.
ALEXANDER	This learning brings a nigger nothing but trouble.
AUGUSTUS	*(claps ALEXANDER on the shoulder)*
	That's all right, old man; I have no quarrel with you. You've fought your battle and now you just want to live out your life in peace. But there's a new breed growing up in this New World — and if the white folks don't give us freedom, we'll fight for it!
OLD PRAYER WOMAN	The Lord knows the time to deliver us from these bonds. He'll come and take us home to Glory. Lord have mercy!
SCIPIO	*(scared)*
	You're talking revolt.

AUGUSTUS   I'm talking truth.

                      (HECTOR enters, a middle-aged Negro dressed
                      in muddy rags. He looks around with wild eyes.
                      There is a dead snake in the net he carries. He
                      wanders up to AUGUSTUS and taps him on
                      the shoulder.)

HECTOR   (holds out his net)

                      I catch snakes:
                      big ones, little ones.
                      I'm going to catch
                      all the snakes in the swamp.

                      (walks over to the PRAYERS)

AUGUSTUS   (looks after him, somehow touched; gentle)

                      Why don't you all sit together?

PHEBE   It's just that —

OLD PRAYER
WOMAN   Fouling the Sabbath day
                      with merriment and carrying on!
                      You better watch out, young man!
                      You ain't big enough to run your own life!
                      Remember: "The Lord is my shepherd!"

SCIPIO   (whispering)

                      It goes on like this every Sunday.
                      They call us sinners

SCIPIO (con't.)	because we don't sit with our heads bowed all day. Now I'm as God-fearing as the rest, but I like to have a little fun once in a while.
PHEBE	They're holding a shout tonight. Miss Amalia allow them so long as there's no preaching.
OLD PRAYER WOMAN	Let the Lord be your shepherd. Nobody's big enough to carry this burden but with the help of Jesus' everlasting love. Too much pride is sinful in the eyes of the Lord.
AUGUSTUS	Where do you get your facts, grandma?
OLD PRAYER WOMAN	"Judge not the Lord with feeble sense!"
AUGUSTUS	Do you know what a white man told me once? "For he who knoweth his Master's will, and doeth it not, shall be beaten with many stripes, and thus have I chastened you." Is that the Lord you're talking about?
OLD PRAYER WOMAN	The Lord works in mysterious ways His wonders to perform.
AUGUSTUS	Here's another quote from the Good Book you might not know:

"Behold the day of the Lord cometh,
and thy spoil shall be divided
in the midst of thee.
For I will gather all nations
against Jerusalem to battle;
and the city shall be taken,
and the women ravished;
and half of the city shall go forth
into captivity; and the residue of the people
shall not be cut off from the city.
Then shall the Lord go forth, and fight
against those nations, as when He fought
in the day of battle."
The Israelites fought for their freedom!
God didn't hand it to them.

OLD PRAYER
WOMAN

Get thee behind me, Satan!

(The PRAYERS take up their chant, more frenzied than ever. During the previous debate, SCYLLA has entered, unseen by AUGUSTUS. She observes him intently. HECTOR wanders over to show her his net.)

HECTOR

I'm gonna get all the snakes in the swamp!
They grow and grow, so many snakes.
But I'll kill them!
I'll kill them all!

(SCYLLA pats HECTOR gently on the back, soothing him, all the while staring at AUGUSTUS, as the lights dim and go out.)

FIFTH SCENE

(Night; SCYLLA's cabin. SCYLLA sits behind a crude table strewn with an assortment of bones, twisted roots, beads, dried corn cobs, and the like. Three squat candles light up her face from below. In the distance can be heard the rhythmic ecstasy of the "shout." PHEBE enters, carrying a small package wrapped in cloth. She looks behind her, knocks at the cabin, steps inside.)

SCYLLA	Sit.
	(PHEBE sits.)
	I know your heart, Phebe. You may smile and bow, but you don't trust me. You see me as evil, when I am only a witness to the evil around us.
PHEBE	I was just trying to protect the girl, Scylla, I didn't mean —
SCYLLA	Protect? It's up to me to protect you.
PHEBE	Like you protected Psyche?
SCYLLA	Psyche fell under the power of new life. The fate we are damned to suffer continues in her child. Don't pity her. But you — I see the spirits around us and I know the forces within us. And you have made the spirits angry.
PHEBE	I never meant no harm —

SCYLLA

Let me see which spirits
you have angered.

*(from a pouch she takes out a forked branch
and arranges the candles in a half-circle around
the branch)*

The body moves through the world.

*(placing a round white stone between the fork
of the branch)*

The mind rests in the body.

*(sprinkles green powder from a vial onto the
branch and the stone)*

The soul is bright
as a jewel, lighter than air.

*(blows the powder away, the candles flare, PHEBE
coughs)*

There is a curse on the land.
The net draws closer.
What have you brought?

*(PHEBE shoves her bundle across the table.
SCYLLA takes it and pulls out a pink ribbon.
She drapes the ribbon over the branch and sprinkles
powder on the first candle.)*

SCYLLA

"Eshu Elewi ogo gbogbo
na mirin ita alagwanna
baba mi mulo no buruku nitosi

le choncho kuele kuikuo
oki kosi eyo!"

(The candle flares and goes out.)

PHEBE   Oh!

SCYLLA   You have tried to make the earth
give up her dead.

*(Reaching into the bundle, she pulls out a necklace
made of shells and drapes it across the branch.
Sprinkling powder on the second candle, she
intones:)*

"kosi eyo,
kosi iku,
kosi ano —"

(The second candle goes out.)

You have tried to snatch spoken words
back from the air. The wind is angry.
It will be hard to satisfy him.

PHEBE   *(desperately)*

What can I do?

SCYLLA   You have made enemies
with two of the mightiest spirits —
Earth and Wind! And these shabby offerings

(indicating the ribbon and necklace)

are supposed to keep them still?

PHEBE

(pulls a white handkerchief out of her pocket)

This... it's from my mama.
There's a little lace on it — see?

(SCYLLA snatches the handkerchief, places it on the branch and repeats the procedure with powder and incantation.)

SCYLLA

"ni oru ko mi gbogbo
omonile fu kuikuo
modupue,
baba mi Elewa."

(The third candle flickers, stays lit.)

Ah!

PHEBE

What is it?

SCYLLA

Are you prepared to hear
what the spirits have to say?

PHEBE

(gathering courage)

If there's something I need to know,
I want to know it.

SCYLLA

You are in great danger.
I give you two warnings.
Guard your footsteps:
they are your imprint on the Earth.
If a sharp stone or piece of glass
falls into the path you have walked,
you will go lame.

Guard your breath:
do not throw with words, because
whenever the wind blows and
your mouth is open,
your soul could be snatched away.

(pauses to let it sink in)

That is all. Go now.

(PHEBE hurries off, shuffling her feet so as to blur her footprints as she flees. On the way to her cabin, she passes AUGUSTUS, who is squatting outside a cabin. He is in ankle chains. In the distance the "shout" can still be heard.)

AUGUSTUS   Evening.

PHEBE   Evening.

(tries to walk past)

AUGUSTUS   What's your hurry? Why don't
you keep me company for a spell?
Unless you're scared of me, too.

PHEBE   Scared of you? Why should
I be scared of you?

AUGUSTUS   *(smiling)*

I can't think of a reason in the world.
Come on, rest yourself.

(PHEBE approaches slowly, sits down beside him carefully)

AUGUSTUS	Sure is a fine night.
	(PHEBE nods.)
	Are you back from the shout?
PHEBE	No.
AUGUSTUS	I didn't think you were the sort who went in for that.
	(scream in the distance)
	Poor souls!
	(looks at PHEBE)
	You're trembling.
PHEBE	I am?
AUGUSTUS	Yes, you are. And I don't believe it's entirely my doing. Fear eats out the heart, you know.
	(looking off)
	Fear: how suddenly it can turn! It can topple the strong as well as the weak. It can make senators and field niggers alike crawl in their own piss. Listen!
	(gesturing in the direction of the "shout")
	God-fearing folk. White-fearing niggers. Death-fearing slaves.

PHEBE	Ain't you scared sometimes?
AUGUSTUS	Of what? White folks? They're more afraid of me. Pain? Every whipping's got to come to an end. Now tell me — what could be worse than walking in chains while others dance?
PHEBE	I heard you've been whipped so many times they lost count.
AUGUSTUS	They thought they could beat me to my senses. But when they looked into my eyes and saw I wasn't afraid, they didn't know what else to do.
PHEBE	It'd be something, not to be afraid.
AUGUSTUS	You have to have a purpose. I have a score to settle and I can't die until it's done.
PHEBE	And nobody ever tried to kill you?
AUGUSTUS	Oh, yes. First time, I was a newborn babe.
	(bitter laugh)
	I was hardly alive.
PHEBE	They whipped you when you was a baby?

AUGUSTUS	Daddy was my massa: the night I was born they took me from my mother, put me in a basket, and galloped away. By the time they stopped to take me out my side was torn open. I didn't walk until I was three. So you see, I met death before I was properly introduced to life.
PHEBE	Lord have mercy.
AUGUSTUS	*(sharply)* Mercy had nothing to do with it. They threw me out like trash.
PHEBE	But a bastard child's still a slave, and a slave has some value. Miss Amalia never seemed to care about Massa's bastard children running around.
AUGUSTUS	*(lost in thought)* I believe Death and I have made a pact. He didn't get me the first time, so this time he'll wait till I'm ready. And I won't be ready until I find the man

who tried to kill me — my father.
Then I will kill him.

(*musing*)

That's how it is: those bounty hunters
and overseers can't do a thing
to me. Do you know what they see
when they look into my eyes?
They see Death, smiling out.

PHEBE   Oh!

AUGUSTUS   You've stopped shaking.
Now why don't you tell me
what made you that way
in the first place?

PHEBE   I can't —

AUGUSTUS   Conjuration, I imagine?
Mumble-jumble from that old woman.

PHEBE   Her name's Scylla.

AUGUSTUS   Women like her, huh!
They get a chill one morning,
hear an owl or two, and
snap! — they've received their "powers"!
Then they collect a few old bones,
dry some herbs, and they're in business.

PHEBE   She told me to watch my footsteps —

AUGUSTUS	— or you'd fall lame.
PHEBE	And to keep my mouth shut when the wind blowed —
AUGUSTUS	— or else the wind spirit would steal your soul.
· PHEBE	(afraid) How'd you know?
AUGUSTUS	You think she's the only conjurer in the world? Why, your Scylla's a baby compared to the voodoo chiefs in the islands. They can kill you with a puff of smoke from their pipe! If you believe in them, that is. Look at me: I carry enough curses on my head to bring a whole ship down around me, but no ship I sailed on ever sank. So if this conjuration is supposed to work, they must be saving me for something special. (PHEBE looks at AUGUSTUS with wonder as the lights slowly dim.)

SIXTH SCENE

(The cotton fields, high noon. JONES strides back and forth, prodding the slower pickers. He looks at the sun, cracks his whip on the ground.)

JONES	Noon!
	(JONES exits, wiping his brow with a huge handkerchief. The slaves sit down to eat their provisions — cornpone, salt pork, and water in a gourd. For a moment there is no sound except the sighs and groans of exhaustion.)
ALEXANDER	I swear on all my years there's nothing I hate so much as cotton. Picking, toting, weighing, tramping: the work keeps coming.
SCIPIO	No end in sight, and that's the truth! *(leans back, hands under head)* Now what I'd fancy is a life at sea. Sun and sky and blue water, with just a sip of rum every once in a while. Augustus, you've been to sea. What's it like?
AUGUSTUS	It ain't the easy life. But it's better than picking cotton.

SCIPIO	But what's it like, man? The closest I been to the sea is Charleston port. All those fine flapping sails and tall masts, cotton bales stacked to heaven, bags of rice and indigo... Did you visit a lot of strange places?
AUGUSTUS	We sailed the West Indies route. Stocked up rum, tobacco and beads... then traded them in Martinique for slaves.
SCYLLA	*(cutting)* Did your massa let you get off the ship?
AUGUSTUS	*(with a sharp look a SCYLLA, sarcastically)* Cap'n Newcastle was a generous massa. *(resuming his story)* But those ports! Sand so white, from far off it looked like spilled cream. Palm trees with coconuts. *(to DIANA)* You ever seen a coconut? *(DIANA shakes her head.)* It's a big brown gourd with hair on it like a dog, and when you break it open sweet milk pours out.

DIANA	What does it taste like?
AUGUSTUS	It tastes like... just coconut. There's nothing like it.
SCYLLA	Your stories stir up trouble, young man.
AUGUSTUS	And why is that?

(PHEBE makes a movement as if to stop him. He motions her back.)

Why, Scylla?
It seems you're the only one
who's riled up.

SCYLLA	You're what we call an uppity nigger. Uppity niggers always trip themselves up.
AUGUSTUS	Are you going to put a curse on me, too? Cross your eyes and wave a few roots in the air until I get on my knees and crawl like a child? Because if you are, I have to say "no thankee, ma'am." Augustus Newcastle does not come under your power.
SCYLLA	Oh, you may dance now, but you will fall. The evil inside you

SCYLLA (con't.)	will send you to your knees and you will crawl, crawl in front of us all!
AUGUSTUS	You feed on the ignorance of others and call it magic. What kind of person works against her own people?
	(The slaves murmur.)
SCYLLA	*(stands up)*
	No need to curse you: you been cursed already.
	(SCYLLA exits. The slaves now turn their full attention to AUGUSTUS.)
AUGUSTUS	When I was in Martinique, I heard tell of an event that changed the fate of our people. Did you know there are slaves who have set themselves free? Taken over the land they used to harvest for others? Shall I tell you how they drove out their white masters and forged their own nation, a nation other nations — white nations — respect?
SCIPIO	*(almost afraid to ask)*
	How?

AUGUSTUS

Santo Domingo, San Domingue, Hispaniola —
three names for an island rising like a
    fortress
from the waters of the Caribbean.
Mountains jut from the sea so steep,
it seems at first there's no place
to set a ship. But if you go
through the Windward Passage and on around
the northwest coast, you'll reach a place
where the land descends to sea
like a giant stone staircase
and there you can land.
An island like most islands,
with more than its share of
sun, wild fruit, mosquitoes...
and slaves, half a million —
slaves to chop sugar, slaves
to pick coffee beans and serve
their French masters in all the ways
we serve our masters here.

(He motions for the other slaves to move in closer,
and they do so.)

One summer, news of a revolution
in the old country
threw the French masters into a sweat.
Each gruesome outrage, each possible
    consequence
was discussed evenings as they leaned
back in their rocking chairs
and slaves served the tall cool drinks.
The slaves served carefully,
but listened with even greater care

AUGUSTUS
(con't.)

to talk of a common people rising
against their rulers. The people of France
had marched against their King,
and as they marched they shouted
three words: Liberty, Equality, Fraternity.
Three words were all the island masters
talked about that summer,
and all summer their slaves
served drinks and listened.

One night a group of slaves
held a secret meeting in the forest.
Eight days, they whispered,
and we'll have our freedom.
Lightning flashed in the hills: Equality.
For eight days tom-toms spoke in the
    mountains:
Liberty, the tom-toms whispered.
Brothers and sisters, the tom-toms sang.
On the eighth day, swift as lightning,
the slaves attacked.

(Unseen by the others, AMALIA enters and stands listening.)

To the sound of tambourines and conch shells
they came down the mountains. They swept
onto the plantations carrying torches
and the long harvest knives, the machetes;
they chopped down white men like sugar cane
and set fire to farmyard and manor.
All the whites who could
boarded ships and fled to America.
For three weeks the flames raged.

When the sun finally broke through
the smoke, it shone upon
a new black nation, the nation of:
Haiti!

(He pauses and looks intently at the faces around him.)

Now do you see,
brothers and sisters,
why they've kept this from us?

AMALIA   A lovely speech.

(The slaves are horrified. AUGUSTUS stands impassive.)

I see you're a poet
as well as a rebel.

JONES   *(rushing in)*
Anything wrong, Miss Jennings?

AMALIA   Not a thing, Jones. Just passing
the time of day with my happy flock.

(to AUGUSTUS)

After you've done your chores
this evening, I want to see you
up at the house.

(strides off)

(Blackout.)

SEVENTH SCENE

(The drawing room of the big house. Twilight filters through the curtains; the frogs have started up in the swamp. AMALIA sits in a wicker chair, a decanter of sherry and a tea service on the table next to her. The evening song of the slaves floats in from the fields, a plaintive air with a compelling affirmation of life, a strange melody with no distinct beat or tune. AMALIA rises and goes to the window and is looking out toward the fields when TICEY, an old fat slave woman, enters.)

TICEY	Miss Amalia?
AMALIA	*(without turning)*
	Yes?
TICEY	That new slave, ma'am — he's standing at the front porch!
AMALIA	Well, show him in.
	(still without turning around)
	Ticey?
TICEY	Yes'm?
AMALIA	You can go to bed now.
TICEY	Yes'm.
	(TICEY exits. A moment later, AUGUSTUS appears in the doorway. Though AMALIA knows he is there, she does not turn around.)

AMALIA	What are they singing?
AUGUSTUS	No words you'd understand. No tune you'd recognize.
AMALIA	And how is it they all sing together?
AUGUSTUS	It just grows.
AMALIA	*(turns around, regaining her disdainful manner)*

You know why I called you
up here, don't you?

(AUGUSTUS is silent.)

AMALIA	Speak!
AUGUSTUS	I told a story.
AMALIA	Go on.
AUGUSTUS	*(shrugs)*

It was a true story.
But I don't believe that was
the reason you summoned me.

AMALIA	Oh, this is a bold nigger indeed! Tells the white folks precisely how he feels, doesn't give a hoot what happens to him!

(AUGUSTUS remains impassive.)

So tell me, Mr. Nigger —
why did I summon you?

AUGUSTUS

You decided to buy a slave
known as a troublemaker, with
twenty-two acts of aggression —

(corrects himself)

now twenty-three —
against his owners.

AMALIA

Go on.

AUGUSTUS

But this particular slave
talks well and is not afraid.
You find him a challenge.
You who have bent so many others
to your will
want to see if you can bend
one more.

AMALIA

I could have had you
flogged to your bones
for what you did today.

AUGUSTUS

(almost gently)

Why didn't you?

(AMALIA leaves the window and sits in the wicker chair, pouring herself a sherry. AUGUSTUS remains standing.)

AMALIA	Were you ever happy, Augustus?
AUGUSTUS	Happy? No.
AMALIA	Never? Not even on the ship, with the whole sea around you?
AUGUSTUS	I was a boy. I felt lucky, not happy.
AMALIA	I read your papers with great interest: "Personal servant to Captain Newcastle of Devonshire, of the schooner Victoria. Ports of call: St. Thomas, Tobago, St. Croix, Martinique —" in other words, a slave ship. You were treated kindly?
AUGUSTUS	(pained) I was.
AMALIA	And did Captain Newcastle allow you to go ashore at St. Thomas, Tobago, St. Croix, Martinique?
AUGUSTUS	Yes.
AMALIA	Could you have stayed aboard if you had wished?
AUGUSTUS	If I had wished.

AMALIA	*(looking off)*

I remember the Haitian revolution;
the whole city was in panic.
Over five hundred French plantation owners
showed up in Charleston harbor that year.

(looking directly at AUGUSTUS)

It was a brilliant revolution.

(looking away again)

I've often wondered why more niggers
don't revolt. How often I've said to myself:
"Amalia, if you had been a slave,
you would most certainly have plotted
an insurrection by now."

(laughs delicately)

But we say
all sorts of things to ourselves.
There's no telling what we'd do
if the moment were there for the taking.

(picking up AUGUSTUS's papers again)

What did you learn under
Captain Newcastle's tutelage?

AUGUSTUS	Reading. Writing. Figures.
AMALIA	What did you have to read?

AUGUSTUS	The Tales of the Greeks.
	Milton. And the Bible.
AMALIA	A varied diet. So you followed
	your captain around, both on and off the
	ship.
	You were there when he plotted courses
	or when he supervised the crew
	loading slaves into the hold.

(*AUGUSTUS is silent.*)

Have you ever heard of the Amistad?

AUGUSTUS   Amistad?

AMALIA   No? So there were things
your gentle captain kept from you.

(*pause*)

You've traveled the Middle Passage —
you know what that means for the cargo.
The slave ship Amistad was three days
off the port of Principe when the slaves,
led by Cinque, an African prince,
rushed out of the hold and attacked
with machetes and harpoons.
The crew was worn out from battling
a storm the night before;
they were no match for the Africans,
driven mad by grief. The white men
were killed and thrown overboard

except for two simple sailors,
who were instructed to steer
the vessel back to Africa.
Cinque was unfamiliar with the stars
in the northern hemisphere;
during the day he set the course
east by the sun, but at night
the two turned the boat around
and steered west.
They continued in this manner,
eastward by day and westward by night,
until one night the sailors managed
to land on our shores.
Cinque and his followers were extradited
to Cuba, where they were executed.

AUGUSTUS   Poor souls.

AMALIA   Why don't more slaves revolt?
Why? Over the years I've come to the
     conclusion
they simply haven't got the guts.
And so they deserve their fate.

AUGUSTUS   I knew a slave once
by the name of Isaac.
Isaac was a gentle man
and there wasn't much in this world
he expected to change, but he held onto
one belief — the Gospel.
When God called him, he was a boy of twelve
out hunting rice birds.
Killing rice birds is easy —

AUGUSTUS
(con't.)

just climb the tree
and pinch off the babies' heads.
Isaac had just spotted a nest of young birds
and was halfway up the tree when
he looked and above him, sitting
in a crook of a branch,
was an angel. "Don't do it, Isaac,"
the angel said. After that,
Isaac began preaching;
he preached patience, understanding,
and leading an innocent life
under the care of God. Massa
let him preach. After all,
what harm could it do?

(takes a deep breath)

Then over in Virginia
a slave uprising one spring
had white people shivering in their beds
and watching their own slaves
for signs of treachery.
Slaves were forbidden to gather
in groups larger than three
for fear of conspiracy.
Isaac was forbidden to hold church service.
But that was one thing Isaac
couldn't understand — the word of God
must be brought to the people
no matter the consequences.
He kept on preaching, at night,
in the woods. And he was caught.

Of the slaves who had prayed with him,
three were shot, three flogged
to death, and one badly wounded.
But what to do about Isaac,
gentle Isaac who had turned traitor?
Killing wasn't good enough.

(takes another deep breath)

First, he was flogged and the wounds
pickled with salt water. When his back
was nearly healed, he was flogged
and his back pickled again.
They kept this up for several months,
and in the meantime, Massa began
to sell off Isaac's children, one at a time.
And when Isaac's back had healed
for the last time, they took him
to see his wife on the auction block,
a baby at her breast. A week later,
wife and children gone, Isaac was sold
to the deep south; but as his new owner
led him from the auction block,
Isaac dropped down dead.

(pause; then more to himself than to AMALIA)

They couldn't break his spirit,
so they broke his heart.

AMALIA   Why are you telling me this?

AUGUSTUS

Trust and patience
are diseases of the soul.
I'm not like Isaac. If I am to be punished,
I will deserve that punishment;
and if I am punished without
deserving it, I will find my revenge.
It's simple: if someone tries
to kill me, I will try to kill him.
If I fail, it is his duty
to kill me. And if for some reason
he decides not to, then I will
continue to live — but I will not
thank him for my life.

AMALIA

(secretly thrilled)

If you had tried to kill a white man
you would surely be dead.

AUGUSTUS

One fine soft night in April
when the pear blossoms
cast their pale faces on
the darker face of the earth,
my mother lay sleeping in her cabin.
On that same fine April night
Massa stood up from the porch swing,
stretched as he gazed at the stars
sprinkled across the brow of heaven,
and thought: "I think I'll make me
another bright-eyed pickaninny,"
and headed for my mother's cabin.
And now that pickaninny,
who started out no more than

the twinkle in his papa's eyes
and the shame between his mama's legs,
is standing in the elegant parlor
of another massa,
entertaining the pretty mistress
with stories of whippings and heartbreak.

AMALIA

(getting up from the chair, going to the window)

The only way to face life is with a grip
on everything you hate and fear.
Half my life I spent dreaming —
the other half burying dreams.

(pause)

Twenty years ago, sickened by life,
my husband withdrew to his rooms
off the upstairs balcony. He studies
the stars. Every night you can see him
there, silk scarf tied at his throat
to ward off a chill.

AUGUSTUS

Sickened by life...

AMALIA

We all deserve our fate.

(AMALIA stares at AUGUSTUS and puts out a hand. He steps toward her. She slowly clasps his forearm. He takes her hair in his hands and kisses her as the CHORUS surges in triumphant song.)

(Blackout.)

EIGHTH SCENE

(It's night. AUGUSTUS waits at the edge of the swamp. He hears a bird call and whistles back. NED appears, a man about AUGUSTUS's age, dressed like a slave but with the mannerisms of a free Negro.)

NED	There you are! We've waited two nights.
AUGUSTUS	I couldn't get away.
NED	No matter. Hurry! *(The lights come up on a room where a group of Black men sit in a semi-circle. NED and AUGUSTUS enter.)*
NED	*(lifting a hand in greeting)* May Fate be with you.
LEADER	*(rising)* And with us all. *(shakes hands with NED, then AUGUSTUS; to NED)* Any trouble?
NED	Not at all. *(AUGUSTUS is led to a small group of initiates as the LEADER looks over the gathering.)*

LEADER	Gentlemen, we have called you here by virtue of your individual acts of resistance against the white race which enslaves our people, thus defying all ideas of democracy and morality. You have proven yourselves firm believers in freedom, warriors willing to risk death for your deeds. For months I have gleaned the city of Charleston and surrounding 　　countryside for men such as yourselves. Each one of us *(indicating the others)* has taken an oath to serve the movement faithfully and to reveal our 　　plans to none, on pain of death. You have been chosen to take this same oath and to enter your names as one of the Band. We are ready. Benjamin Skeene?
BENJAMIN	*(stepping forward)* Yes, sir?
LEADER	Are you prepared to slay our oppressors, male and female, when it is deemed time, according to the plans of insurrection drawn up and approved by members present?
BENJAMIN	I am. *(signs his name in the book)*

80

LEADER	Henry Blake?
	(HENRY steps forward hesitantly.)
	Are you prepared to slay our oppressors, male and female, when it is deemed time, according to the plans of insurrection drawn up and approved by members present?
HENRY	I'm a religious man...
LEADER	"...and the children of Israel sighed by reason of the bondage, and they cried, and their cry came up unto God by reason of the bondage. And God heard their groaning, and God remembered his covenant with Abraham, with Isaac, and with Jacob."
HENRY	I'm against the white man as much as all of you, but... murder? Killing all, without difference, women and children? "Thou shalt not kill," saith the Commandments.
LEADER	"Behold, the day of the Lord cometh, and thy spoil shall be divided in the midst of thee. For I will gather all nations against Jerusalem to battle:

LEADER (con't.)	and the city shall be taken, and the houses rifled, and the women ravished; and half of them shall go forth into captivity. Then shall the Lord go forth and fight against those nations, as when he fought in the days of battle." *(pause)* Are you prepared to sign your name with the revolutionary forces?
HENRY	I... I...
LEADER	*(threatening)* We cannot risk betrayal. Refusal will mean... *(HENRY signs the book.)* Augustus Newcastle? *(AUGUSTUS steps forward with determination.)* We have followed your actions with great interest. It gladdens us that Providence has seen fit to bring you to this part of the land. Are you prepared to slay

	our oppressors, male and female, when it is deemed time, according to the plans of insurrection drawn up and approved by members present?
AUGUSTUS	I am.
	(signs the book)
	(The old members rise and shake hands with the new members. They all sit down as the LEADER prepares to speak again.)
LEADER	It is time we had our liberty. The white man has shown no intention of granting this freedom — indeed, the very notion seems inconceivable to him, inasmuch as he regards our men as little more than beasts of burden and all too often regards our women as his personal instruments of pleasure. We then, have determined to take Fate into our own hands. Hence our password: "May Fate be with you — and with us all." Our intention is simple: to free ourselves even if we must die in the attempt. Plans are under way. We are not alone in our struggle — our free brothers are also willing to make sacrifices for their brothers in bondage. In the community, one is fashioning daggers at his smithy.

LEADER (con't.)   Barrels of gun powder have been stored
in caches outside the city
in readiness for the big battle.
One of our members has procured
a metal mold, and is in the process of
producing cannon balls, which are stored
under water near the dock.
The night destined to change history
is not far off.

(pause)

Maps of the city are being drawn up
with points of attack
but in the interest of security
will not be distributed until later.
For the same reason, the exact date
will not be announced until immediately
beforehand. We cannot take chances.
I caution — trust no one.
Sow discontent among other Negroes,
but in no wise attempt to recruit members
or reveal any aspect of the plot
until we have all had opportunity
to observe the promising candidate
and reach a decision.

(significantly)

All those who are not with us
are against us, Blacks as well
as whites. And so I warn you:

do not falter. Strengthen your resolve
with the memory of the atrocities
    committed
against your mothers and daughters,
the cruel punishments inflicted upon
your fathers and sons. Go to your people
and test their minds: gird them for battle
with ideas, so when the fires lick
the skies of Charleston, they will
rise up of one accord,
knowing the day of revenge has come!

ALL   *(rise and embrace as they sing)*

Steal away, steal away,
Steal away to Jesus;
Steal away, steal away home,
I ain't got long to stay here.

(Blackout.)

NINTH SCENE

(The cottonhouse: the SLAVES are tramping down the cotton. The dull thud of stomping feet punctuates the dialogue, changes in pace and rhythm signaling changes in mood and tension. ALEXANDER looks out the one small window.)

ALEXANDER	There he goes.
OLD PRAYER WOMAN	Every evening, same time. It's the devil's work afoot, for sure.
SCIPIO	Peculiar it is! I wonder —
PHEBE	*(snapping)* It ain't your task to wonder.
ALEXANDER	What's the matter with you, gal? Most times you're the one speculating about other folks' doings.
SCIPIO	Maybe Phebe's sweet on him. *(The others laugh.)*
PHEBE	*(flaring)* If you all ain't finding fault with someone, you're laughing at them! We've all been called up to the house one time or another. Ain't nothing special in that.

SCYLLA	For two weeks in a row? As soon as the sun eases into the sycamores there ain't a hair of his to be seen till daylight. (*significant pause*) Except maybe on his lady's pillow.
PHEBE	What you trying to say, Scylla?
SCYLLA	(*evenly*) I ain't trying to say nothing.
ALEXANDER	(*timidly*) He's certainly the boldest nigger I've ever seen.
SCIPIO	That's the truth there! (*shaking his head in admiration*) The way he handles Massa Jones — no bowing or scraping for him. That eye of his could cut through stone. (*chuckles*) Jones don't know what to do with that nigger! He's plain scared, and that's a fact.

DIANA	Augustus is nice.
OLD PRAYER WOMAN	Nice as the devil was to Eve.
PHEBE	*(lamely)* Maybe they're just talking.
SCYLLA	A slave and his missus ain't got nothing to talk about. Oh, he might have bold ideas, but he'll never put them to work. She'll see to that.
PHEBE	What do you mean?
SCYLLA	When he was a boy, that first master of his kept him in style. He grew accustomed to being petted. That's why afterwards he ran away so much: He ain't used to being treated like a regular slave, and he'll never get used to it. A whip can't make him behave: Miss Amalia knows that. So she's trying another way. *(nods toward the house)* It seems to be working.

SCIPIO	Well, I'll be — that thought never crossed my mind.
PHEBE	Oh, Scylla, I can't believe it. He just wouldn't! With Miss Amalia? No, it can't be!
ALEXANDER	What 'pears to be working?
SCYLLA	Now what's the only thing white folks think a nigger buck's good for?
ALEXANDER	If that's what he's doing, he's headed for big trouble.
PHEBE	If that's true, it's 'cause he ain't got no choice!
SCYLLA	You been mighty contrary lately, Phebe.
PHEBE	I ain't afraid of every shadow!
SCIPIO	(trying to avert disaster)
	Scylla, don't mind her. She's feeling the weather.
SCYLLA	I'm warning you, Phebe.
PHEBE	I already got a pack of curses on my head. A few more won't hurt.

ALEXANDER	Phebe! Don't talk to Scylla like that!
PHEBE	Should have done it a long time ago. Woman had me nearly crazy, clamping up my mouth anytime the wind blew, wiping out my footsteps so I ended up getting nowhere. If anyone around here's putting sharp stones in my footprints, it ain't no earth spirit. If there's a curse here, Scylla, it's you. *(Everyone stops stamping.)*
DIANA	*(afraid)* Phebe…
PHEBE	Yes, Scylla, you're the curse — with all your roots and potions. Tell me: how come you never put a spell on Miss Amalia? Why didn't you sprinkle some powder over a candle to make her house go up in flames one night? That would have been some magic. *(The others murmur timidly.)*
SCYLLA	I do what the spirits tell me.
PHEBE	Then those Blacks in Haiti must have known some better spirits.

PHEBE (con't.)	*(laughter, agreeing murmurs; SCYLLA realizes the tide is turning against her)*
SCYLLA	Some nigger comes in here with a few pretty stories and you think he's the Savior!
OLD PRAYER WOMAN	Dear Lord!
PHEBE	The Savior was never to your liking, Scylla. He took too much attention away from you.
OLD PRAYER WOMAN	Have mercy!
SCYLLA	There's a vine in the woods with a leaf like a saw blade. One leaf-side is shiny dark and pocked like skin; the other side is dusty gray. Touch the gray side to a wound, the sore will shut and heal. But touch it with the shiny side, and the wound will boil up and burst open.
PHEBE	Always talking in riddles! Why don't you come right out and say what you mean for a change?

(Consenting murmurs; SCYLLA draws herself up and looks darkly at them until they grow silent. PHEBE is trembling at her own boldness.)

SCYLLA

Alright, I'll tell you direct.
Your Augustus is a pretty clever nigger —
been lots of places and knows
the meanings of words and things like that.
But something's foul in his blood.
He may 'pear to be a budding flower,
but there's a worm
eating away at the root.
What's festering inside him
nothing this side of the living
can heal. And when a body's
hurting that bad, a person lose sight of
what's good or evil. They do anything
to get relief — anything.

(looking around at all of them)

So go ahead and follow your man.
Keep talking about Haiti
and sharpening your sticks!
But know one thing —
that nigger's headed for destruction,
and you're all headed there with him.

(They stare at her as the lights dim to blackout.)

T E N T H   S C E N E

(The edge of the swamp. HECTOR is alone, covered with mud and carrying his net. He is searching among the reeds.)

HECTOR

So many! Under rocks and twixt reeds.
They lie and breed, breed, breed
until they get me out of bed.
The wicked never rest.

(stops, listens)

What's that? Someone coming?

(hides)

(NED and AUGUSTUS enter. They shake hands.)

NED

Good night, friend. It was a golden day
when Fate brought you to us.

AUGUSTUS

We will be victorious.

(NED exits.)

HECTOR

You!
I seen you before.

AUGUSTUS

(whirls around; then, relieved)

That you have, my friend.
I'm one of the Jennings
plantation slaves, like you.

HECTOR

What are you doing in my swamp?

AUGUSTUS   Taking a walk. Breathing the night air.

HECTOR   Wrong! You were with someone.
            I saw you!

AUGUSTUS   A friend, Hector. Don't you have friends?

HECTOR   (suspicious)

            How do you know my name?

AUGUSTUS   (impatient)

            I've heard of you — I told you,
            I'm a slave here, too.
            Miss Amalia bought me last —

HECTOR   Amalia!

            (pause)

            You plotting some evil.

AUGUSTUS   You've got swamp fever, old man.
            I plan no evil.

HECTOR   I heard you!
            You are planning a great evil.
            Men come and go in wagons.
            They whisper and shake hands.
            They come out at night
            when the innocent sleep.

AUGUSTUS	You are mad, man.
HECTOR	*(shouting)*
	You are one of them! But I won't let you hurt her! I won't let you hurt her!
AUGUSTUS	Quiet! Someone might hear.
HECTOR	*(shouting louder)*
	Help! Help! Danger! Wake up, wake up, a great danger —
	(AUGUSTUS grabs him; they struggle and fall to the ground. AUGUSTUS quickly gains control and chokes HECTOR. He rolls the body into the swamp. He reemerges, sweating and wild.)
AUGUSTUS	*(listening)*
	No one's coming.
	(pause)
	They're sleeping like lambs.
	(His bitter laugh turns to a sob.)
	Damn you, old man, I had no choice. "Who is not with us, is against us."
	(hesitates, then runs off)
	(Blackout.)

ELEVENTH SCENE

(Early evening, AMALIA's bedroom. AMALIA kneels before the fire-place, trying to start it. She burns her hand, curses softly. TICEY rushes in.)

TICEY	Miss Amalia! That's my job! Did you burn yourself?
AMALIA	*(hiding her hand)* No.
TICEY	Ain't no job for a lady. I'll have this room nice and toasty quick as you can snap your fingers.
AMALIA	*(softly)* I was just trying to see what it's like.
TICEY	*(preoccupied with the fire)* Beg pardon, Ma'am?
AMALIA	Nothing. If only this weather would break!
TICEY	I know what you mean, ma'am. Three days of this chill is three days too much for my poor old bones.

AMALIA	A cold snap, that's all. The season will right itself soon enough.
TICEY	Yes'm.
AMALIA	(gently) You've worked hard, Ticey. Go and enjoy the evening.
TICEY	(amazed) Yes'm. Thank you, ma'am! (exits)
AMALIA	(curls up by the fireplace) The princess said to her father, "Bring me strawberries, I am hungry for strawberries." He came back with a husband instead. "I'm getting too old to tend the garden," the King said. "Here is a husband for you — he will fetch your strawberries." The princess stomped her foot and replied if she must have a husband, she would rather marry the fox, who at least knew where the sweetest berries grew. And without another word the princess ran out of the palace and into the woods. She was frightened at her own daring,

and yet she ran on and on
until a pebble in her shoe forced her to stop.
But it was not a pebble at all —
it was the King's head, shrunk to the size
    of a pea.
"Put me in your pocket,"
the King pleaded, "and take me with you."
Appalled, the princess threw the head down
and ran on. But she had not gone far
before she had to stop again,
and this time when she shook out her shoe,
it was the head of her husband that said
"Please put me in your pocket
so I may go with you." The princess
threw this head down, too, and ran faster;
but before long her shoe stopped her
for the third time. And now
it was her own head
she held in her hands.
She cradled it in cupped palms
and cried and cried
until, whimpering, she fell asleep
beneath a giant oak tree.
And so she perished in the deep woods
and her body was never found,
even to this day.

(silence; suddenly she sits up, listening)

Augustus?

(AUGUSTUS enters. AMALIA runs to embrace him.)

AMALIA	So you've come after all. See how good I was to let you go off without asking why. Most women would suspect you had another sweetheart tucked away.
AUGUSTUS	Giving everyone a free evening is hardly the thing to do if you suspect me of that.
AMALIA	I thought if you were too busy to see me, then I need to give you a little more free time. But now you're here — come and get warm. *(leads him to the fire)*
AUGUSTUS	*(testing her)* Cold weather's hard on the crops. They should be picked fast.
AMALIA	*(gaily)* The weather will break. I predict tomorrow!
AUGUSTUS	*(amazed)* Everyone's a prophet around here.
AMALIA	*(sitting)* Scylla says the day will break warm.

AUGUSTUS	*(remains standing)*
	Since when have you taken to consulting Scylla?
AMALIA	I didn't "consult" her. She came up to me today and said, "If it please the Mistress, the cold has run its course. Morn will break warm, no worry." Funny woman!
AUGUSTUS	Why should you risk your profit on Scylla's words?
AMALIA	What risk? Scylla's always been right before.

(AUGUSTUS stands as if changed into stone.
AMALIA leans against his thigh.)

Let's make up fables.

(gazing into the fire)

We are brother and sister ruling
a ravished country. Our subjects lie
in the doorways of their ruined houses
too weak to fend off the flies
feeding on their sores. Pigs have broken loose
and are roaming the streets.
Once, a long time ago,
we could have moved our kingdom
into a fertile valley and averted
catastrophe, but we were afraid.
And now it is too late.

AMALIA (con't.)	*(With a pained expression, AUGUSTUS places his hands on top of her hair, as if in blessing.)*
	Each day we see suffering and suffer because we are the cause. From time to time we step out onto the royal balcony to show ourselves to the people so that they will have someone to blame, someone to plot against.
AUGUSTUS	You're a strange lady.
AMALIA	Now it's your turn. A fable!
AUGUSTUS	What about?
AMALIA	Tell me how you got your scars.
AUGUSTUS	Again?
AMALIA	Not "again"! Do you think I believe that tale about you being Apollo's favorite?
AUGUSTUS	You're right. I wasn't favored by Apollo. I was his son.
AMALIA	Augustus!
AUGUSTUS	No, it's true. My mother was a beautiful Nubian

who had thrilled the sun god so much
he granted her one wish.
So she wished that he might
leave his mark on his new offspring.
As Apollo gave his blessing,
he stroked a finger along my side
and the words he spoke over my cradle
burned themselves into my memory
as if they had always been stirring
inside me. "To the rest of the world,"
he said, "these may be scars;
but to you they shall be
the mark of royalty,
for you are my son and my light."

(pulls up his shirt to expose his side)

Don't they look like crowns?

AMALIA

They look more like suns —
exploding suns.

AUGUSTUS

Actually, I wasn't Apollo's legitimate son;
I was his bastard and stable boy.
Every evening he drove his two gallant
    steeds
up to the Olympian stables
and gave them into my care.
They stood calmly while I wiped
the sparkling froth from their mouths
and eased each golden bit and bridle.
I combed their fiery manes
and smoothed their pale coats.

AUGUSTUS
(con't.)

Then one morning Apollo appeared with
his legitimate son, whose name was Phaëthon.
Apollo had foolishly promised him
anything his heart desired,
and Phaëthon's heart wished
nothing less than to drive
the chariot of the sun for one day.
Apollo instantly regretted his rash promise
but a god's word is law
and the boy was stubborn.
After careful instruction, Apollo
reluctantly left us.

I had not noticed
that on his slender feet Phaëthon had slipped
a pair of golden spurs.
As I lifted my half-brother up,
he squirmed and accidentally kicked me
with the spurs. Surprised by pain, I dropped
    him
into the chariot — and the horses,
frightened by the jolt,
dashed into the heavens
before the boy had a chance to catch the
    reins.

That was a terrible day.
I lay in a swoon until Hermes,
always the first to know anything,
passed by and saw my predicament.
He alerted Zeus, who darkened with anger

and sent for Apollo, but Apollo had already
raced off in search of Phaëthon.

Apollo returned that evening with the horses
but without his son. It seems
the runaway chariot had swooped
too near the earth, scorching a continent
and blackening the skin of its people
so that Zeus was forced to strike
the chariot with a thunderbolt
to avert further disaster;
Phaëthon plunged into the sea,
and Zeus foretold the abduction and
enslavement of these dark people.

When the time came for the prophecy
to be fulfilled, I went to Apollo
and asked to be sent down to earth
in order to live among the unfortunates
whose fate was enmeshed with mine.
"Give me a human form
and the memory of my origins,"
I asked, "and the promise that
when I die, I can return to Olympus
as your stable boy."
All of which Apollo granted.

AMALIA   So what is your mission on earth?

AUGUSTUS   I am sworn to secrecy.

AMALIA	*(reaching for AUGUSTUS)*
	It's getting late.
	(AUGUSTUS takes AMALIA in his arms. They look at each other. The SLAVES begin softly humming "Steal Away.")
AUGUSTUS	Ah, little Missy...
	(kisses her)
	Will they miss me if I don't take my place out there under the stars tonight?
	(The strains of "Steal Away" grow louder and more urgent, but AUGUSTUS appears not to hear. He and AMALIA embrace as the lights dim.)

TWELFTH SCENE

(HECTOR's funeral. HECTOR's body is lying in state on a crude plat-
form, covered with a rough blanket. The SLAVES march around the
bier as they sing.)

CHORUS

Oh Deat' him is a little man,
And him goes from do' to do',
Him kill some souls and him cripple up,
And him lef' some souls to pray.

Do Lord, remember me,
Do Lord, remember me;
I cry to the Lord as de year roll aroun',
Lord, remember me.

I want to die like-a Jesus die,
And he die wid a free good will,
I lay out in de grave and I stretch out de
    arms,
Do, Lord, remember me.

ALEXANDER

His children scattered
around this world.

PHEBE

We're all his friends, Alexander.

ALEXANDER

But his youngest child's got to
pass over and under the grave!
Who's going to do it?

PHEBE	Every child on this plantation was like his child, Alexander. The youngest of them will pass under. Don't you worry.
ALEXANDER	(breaking down) To die swoll up and burst open like a —
PHEBE	He's at rest now. He don't feel it.

(The SLAVES stop marching to prepare for the ritual of the "passing." In this rite, the youngest child of the deceased is passed under and over the coffin to signify the continuity of life.)

CHORUS

Dese all my fader's children.
Dese all my fader's children,
Dese all my fader's children,
Outshine de sun.

My fader's done wid de trouble o' de world,
Wid de trouble o' de world,
Wid de trouble o' de world,
My fader's done wid de trouble o' de world,
Outshine de sun.

(During the ceremony, AUGUSTUS appears and stands uncertainly at the edge of the mourners. PHEBE goes up to him.)

PHEBE	Where were you?
AUGUSTUS	I came soon as I heard —
PHEBE	Not here, man. There.

(She gestures toward the swamp. AUGUSTUS looks terrified.)

They were calling for you last night.
Didn't you hear that "Steal Away?"

AUGUSTUS	I... don't... remember.

PHEBE

They sang till I thought
the dead would rise out their graves
and follow! I was crazy with worry.
"Where's Augustus?" I said to myself,
"Can't he hear they're calling him to
    meeting?"
Finally I went and told them
you were being watched
and couldn't get away.

DIANA

(with the mourners)

Augustus looks sad.

SCIPIO

He's carrying a heavy burden,
child. He's making sure
none of us will have to die
like vermin ever again.

ALEXANDER	None of Hector's children is here any more, but your good mama, Diana — may she rest in peace — was his friend once. You should be the one. *(ALEXANDER and SCIPIO lift DIANA up and pass her under and over the coffin.)*
AUGUSTUS	*(to himself)* I couldn't risk it.
PHEBE	*(not hearing AUGUSTUS)* You can't fool with them, man! If you lose their trust, you're dead. What's gotten into you?
AUGUSTUS	*(to himself)* A traitor is a traitor.
PHEBE	You are a leader! You came to us and made us see there's a way to freedom. We'll die if necessary — but with dignity. Remember that. *(PHEBE returns to the mourners and AUGUSTUS sits down, too tired to stand any longer. SCYLLA approaches, ravaged with grief and more stooped than ever.)*
SCYLLA	He was a good man.

AUGUSTUS	*(wearily)*
	Yes. He was good.
SCYLLA	And you are evil.
AUGUSTUS	You've said that before.
SCYLLA	Don't make the mistake of thinking I'm a fool. I am patient and alert. And I can smell death's sour breath all over you.
AUGUSTUS	Don't come around me, then.
SCYLLA	You believe you can cure the spirit just by riling it. But the spirit needs more. You give these people nothing but hate. What are they going to do with your hate after you free them... as you promise?
AUGUSTUS	I won't argue anymore with you, Scylla. I've got things to do.
SCYLLA	*(triumphant)*
	Yes, you're busy. You have to watch out for people waiting to trip you up. You think the danger's on the outside, but do you know what's inside you, Augustus? The seeds of the future. They'll have their way. You can't escape: you are in your skin wherever you go.
	(Blackout.)

THIRTEENTH SCENE

(Late afternoon. PHEBE and AUGUSTUS are standing before the slave cabins. AUGUSTUS is agitated.)

AUGUSTUS	Everything ready?
PHEBE	Yes.
AUGUSTUS	You've been careful?
PHEBE	What kind of fool you think I am?
AUGUSTUS	I expect the call any time now.
PHEBE	It's been three days, Augustus.
AUGUSTUS	Tonight! Tonight we'll show the white man how well we've learned his brand of justice. We'll blow up his bridges and burn his palaces and kill his pale sons.
PHEBE	*(touch of sarcasm)* We're ready and waiting, Augustus. All you have to do is say the word.

AUGUSTUS	Our day of reckoning is here!
PHEBE	Are you sure it's not just your day?
AUGUSTUS	What do you mean?
PHEBE	Every time you talk about our day, our victory, our vengeance, it's as if you're saying my day, my victory, my vengeance. As if you didn't care about anyone's pain but yours.
AUGUSTUS	I'm risking my life, and this is how you thank me!
PHEBE	Don't think bad of me, Augustus. I'm grateful for what you've done to change my way of thinking, and the others are, too. But sometimes I look at you and wonder where the real Augustus is. Sometimes I catch a glimpse of him, behind those fine speeches and mighty shoulders; sometimes he's peeking out from way down inside, a gentle boy with eyes that see too much. Sometimes when you come back from the house —
AUGUSTUS	Shut up, woman!

PHEBE

Ain't nothing wrong with feelings,
Augustus, just where they lead you to.
Now, when it comes to hating,
you and Miss Amalia are a lot alike.

(AUGUSTUS whirls on her, but she stands her ground.)

When her father was still living
she was different, cheerful,
always ready to laugh. But from the time
she married Massa Louis,
she began to sour, and after
she lost the baby it seemed like
disappointment killed her. And now
you've brought her back to life.
No wonder you're mixed up!
No one can look at changes he's caused
without feeling funny.

AUGUSTUS

Why are you saying this now,
when I need all the hate in my power
to do what I have to do?

PHEBE

Because I care what happens to you
more than revolution or making history.
Those may be traitor's words, but I don't
    care.
'Cause maybe... maybe, if
you hadn't let hate take over your life,
you would have had some love
left over for me.

(PHEBE runs off. AUGUSTUS stands still for a moment, as if a new and treacherous path had opened before him. He slowly sits down and buries his face in his hands.)

AUGUSTUS

They'll drive us into the sea.
They'll turn this boat around
and lead us to slaughter.

(The conspirators NED and BENJAMIN enter.)

NED

There he is. Doesn't look
so fearful now, does he?

BENJAMIN

I figured there couldn't be a slave
tough as he was claimed to be —
not alive, there couldn't.
What if he's said something already?

NED

He hasn't done anything yet,
but we'll have to be careful.
We'll double-check everything
he's assigned to do.

AUGUSTUS

Who's there?

NED

May Fate be with you.

AUGUSTUS

(rising)

And with all of us.
You've brought news?

BENJAMIN

Most of the news is old, brother.

AUGUSTUS	It couldn't be helped; I'm under constant guard. To leave the plantation would have aroused suspicion.
NED	(sarcastic) Constant guard? Constant companionship would be closer to the truth.
AUGUSTUS	Talk straight.
NED	As straight as I can, brother. You missed a very important meeting, sent word that you were "being watched" — those were the words, brother. Naturally, we were concerned. Naturally, we sent someone to check up on your difficulties. Think of our surprise when we found out who your guard was, and how tenderly she watched over you!
AUGUSTUS	Scylla told you!
BENJAMIN	So you admit it? You confess your treachery just like that? We expected a bit more finesse.
AUGUSTUS	Missy needed a buck — what of it? We've all had to dance to that piper one time or another. She piped, I went. Missy wants, Missy gets.
BENJAMIN	Sound mighty proud, buck.

AUGUSTUS	Just the facts, brother. Just facts.
	Should I knock her hand away, curse her
	to prove my loyalty to the cause?
	Why not charm her instead —
	play the love-sick nigger
	ready and willing to wash her feet
	with the sweat from his brow?
	What better way to divert suspicion?
NED	That never used to be your tactic.
AUGUSTUS	I never had such a clear
	chance for freedom.
NED	All the more reason to see
	you don't spoil it.
	(comes to a decision)
	The night's perfect:
	overcast, new moon.
	We can operate in total darkness.
AUGUSTUS	Tonight? I'll have to assemble
	my fighters. What shall I tell them?
	Quick, give me details.
NED	Hold on. You'll be coming with us.
AUGUSTUS	I just told you —

NED	You told us what you wanted us to believe. We need more proof.
AUGUSTUS	Then what —
NED	Our orders are to bring you with us. Your second-in-command can organize things here.
AUGUSTUS	I can't leave. They need me!
BENJAMIN	This is death's business, brother. Even a nigger as famous as you can't be given the benefit of the doubt!
NED	Where's the woman who came to us before?
AUGUSTUS	*(dazed)* Phebe? Second cabin from the end.
NED	*(to BENJAMIN)* Tell her Augustus has gone to central command and she's to take over. I'll wait for you in the wagon. *(to AUGUSTUS)* Come on. *(All exit. Blackout.)*

FOURTEENTH SCENE

(Twilight, same day. AMALIA's room. AMALIA is seated. PHEBE enters just as SCYLLA is leaving. PHEBE looks after SCYLLA.)

PHEBE	You wanted me, ma'am?
AMALIA	Yes, Phebe, I did. As I sat here wondering what my slaves were making of such a fine Sunday, I happened to look out and see you walking along, talking to this slave and that as you strolled from group to group. I thought to myself, "Maybe Phebe would talk to me, too."
PHEBE	*(on her guard)* I'm pleased to talk conversation whenever you like, Miss Amalia.
AMALIA	*(slightly sarcastic)* It seems you're pleased with other people's conversations these days.
PHEBE	I don't follow your meaning, ma'am.
AMALIA	Oh you don't? I notice you and Augustus have no problem following each other's meaning.

PHEBE	Augustus ain't nothing but a friend, ma'am. I don't recollect talking to him any more than anyone else. *(laughs nervously)* Me and my big mouth always be yakking at somebody or another.
AMALIA	Phebe, don't talk yourself into trouble.
PHEBE	Beg pardon, ma'am. I didn't mean nothing by it.
AMALIA	Everyone can see you're making a fool of yourself over him! *(calms down with an effort)* How long have you been on this plantation, Phebe?
PHEBE	Miss Amalia, you know I was borned here. *(softer)* My mama grew up on this here piece of land.

AMALIA	Your mother was an obedient nigger.
	That's why my daddy saw fit to keep her.
PHEBE	Yes, ma'am.
AMALIA	Have you talked to Augustus today?
PHEBE	I can't say that I did, ma'am.

(at a warning look from AMALIA)

That is — I talked to a lot of people
and he was amongst them, but
we didn't say more than a how-de-do.

AMALIA	Go tell Augustus I want to see him.
PHEBE	*(thrown into panic)*

I don't know — I mean, I can't —

AMALIA	What's wrong, Phebe?
PHEBE	Nothing, ma'am.
	It might take a while, is all.
AMALIA	*(sarcastic)*

And why, pray, is that?

PHEBE	It's just that — well,
	Augustus been keeping to himself lately.
	I remember seeing him going off

PHEBE (con't.)	in the direction of the swamp. He's got some crazy idea about fixing up Hector's shack for himself.
AMALIA	*(haunted)* When he returns, send him up. *(PHEBE exits. In the hallway she runs into AUGUSTUS. He is very agitated.)*
PHEBE	You!
AUGUSTUS	They sent me back. I've got a job to do.
PHEBE	Oh, I was so scared! When Benjamin came and told me to take charge, I thought they were going to kill you. So tell me, what's the plan?
AUGUSTUS	This one I do alone.
PHEBE	Ah. But can you go in there first and calm her down? She thinks we're sweethearts!
AUGUSTUS	*(distracted, very upset)* I've got a job to do.

PHEBE	Augustus? Augustus, are you listening? Whatever they sent you back to do can't be so important that you can't take a minute to smooth that she-hawk's feathers down so's the rest of us can carry out our —

(AMALIA steps out of her room and peers into the dim hall. AUGUSTUS shrinks into the shadows.)

AMALIA	Is that you, Phebe?
PHEBE	Yes'm. I was just on my way downstairs.
AMALIA	I heard voices.
PHEBE	That was me, ma'am. I twisted my foot in the dark — guess I was talking to it.

(laughs nervously)

My mama used to say it helps
to talk the hurt out.

AMALIA	Well, do your talking elsewhere. Go on!

(PHEBE hesitates, then exits. AMALIA stands looking into the darkness for a moment, then thinks better of it and goes back into her room. AUGUSTUS steps out of his hiding place.)

AUGUSTUS

It must be done.
I must do it.

*(He steels himself and heads for LOUIS's room.
The light comes up on LOUIS, sitting in a chair
looking out on the evening sky. LOUIS is wrapped
in a dressing gown and seems frail. His back is
to AUGUSTUS who hesitates at the doorway.)*

LOUIS

No one has come through
that door for years. I've waited.
I sit by the window and if
I listen hard I can hear them
joke and sing — Scipio, Alexander,
Phebe, and now the little girl...

(spins around to face AUGUSTUS)

You're the new one.
Since Amalia bought you
I've been watching you.

(gestures around him)

There's peace in this room.
It's as if I had never existed
outside these walls, as if
the world outside was only my dream.

(gestures towards the heavens)

Beware the Moon in the house of Mars!

(conversationally)

The stars can tell you everything,
you know. Not the details, of course,
just the results: war and pestilence,
love and jealousy, betrayal —
but no date and place, no names.
May I learn your name?

AUGUSTUS

Augustus.

LOUIS

Augustus. A good name.
Strong. A name like Augustus
I could have lived up to, grown into
like a pair of riding breeches.
That's what Amalia needed — a man
to take charge of her.

(looks off into the distance)

A man should be able to kill
when he has to.
Love is as good a reason
as any other, don't you agree?

*(AUGUSTUS has started moving toward him
but halts.)*

Valuable property!
I should have killed the bastard, if only
to give you a reason for revenge —
a heavenly purpose.

AUGUSTUS

Killed whom?

LOUIS

The baby, of course.

AUGUSTUS

What are you talking about?
Speak up!

LOUIS

No one would have been the wiser.

(looks at AUGUSTUS)

How stupid to leave it up to chance!
"It's a long hard ride into town
and so much can happen on the way..."

AUGUSTUS

(grabs the arms of LOUIS's chair and leans over him)

What ride?

LOUIS

Amalia wanted to sell the baby.
I couldn't kill him with my own hands,
and the doctor refused.
What else was there to do?

AUGUSTUS

(shakes the chair)

Go on!

LOUIS

It was a beautiful sewing basket —
lined in blue satin and trimmed
with red rosettes, the kind ladies use
to store their embroidery.
My spurs slipped right in...

(AUGUSTUS lets the chair go slowly)

But the doctor returned the next morning.
"Fool!" he said. "The child's still alive —"

AUGUSTUS	— and still lives to this day.
LOUIS	Entirely possible.
AUGUSTUS	Spurs bite into a horse's belly.

Would you like to see what spurs can do
to the belly of a new-born child?

(pulls open his shirt)

LOUIS	You —
AUGUSTUS	You threw me out like trash,

but I refused to die.
All my life I swore I would find
the white man who did this to me —
find him and kill him.
I had almost given up. And tonight,
sent here by my brothers
on the eve of reckoning,
I have found him.

All these years I tried to imagine
what you would look like.
Would you be tall, or stocky,
or stooped over? Would your eyes
be pale or an ordinary shade of brown?
Would you dress in white linen
like a gentleman

AUGUSTUS
(con't.)

or dash around in a dusty greatcoat?
I never expected a coward. To think
that your blood flows through my veins —

LOUIS

What?

AUGUSTUS

— is the greatest shame.
When I think of you whimpering,
pale as a fish, when I think of you
forcing your wretched seed into
my mother, I want to rip you —

LOUIS

You think I'm your father?

AUGUSTUS

I heard it from your own lips.

LOUIS

(bursts into laughter)

Of course! Of course!
The stars said it all:
who is born to violence
will live to fulfill it.
Who shuns violence
will die by the sword.

AUGUSTUS

My mother — what did you do to her?

LOUIS

Your mother?

(laughs)

AUGUSTUS

(pulls LOUIS out of his chair and shakes him)

Where is my mother?

LOUIS

(in a crafty voice)

I haven't touched her since.
Why don't you ask Amalia?
She runs this plantation. Ask her.
She knows your mother quite well!

(There is a sudden shout outside; the revolt has begun. Both men freeze, listening.)

AUGUSTUS

No time!

(Seized by desperation, he chokes LOUIS. The sounds of the revolt grow. Finally, AUGUSTUS stands above the body. He speaks with malignant jubilation.)

AUGUSTUS

So, Amalia, you kept this story
to yourself. To think an hour ago
I tried to bargain for your life!
They were right not to trust me.
"Kill them both," they said,
"your mistress and her foolish husband."
Proof, they said. They needed proof
I had not betrayed the cause.

(There are shouts and cheers outside. AUGUSTUS heads for AMALIA's room. The lights come up on AMALIA, who has stepped into the hall.)

AMALIA

Ticey? Ticey,
where are you?
Come here this minute!

AMALIA (con't.)	*(She sees AUGUSTUS and breaks off her cry. She runs towards him but stops short at the sight of his face.)* Augustus, there you are! I tried ringing, but Ticey won't come! *(AUGUSTUS walks toward her, backing her into the bedroom.)* What's happening, Augustus? That noise outside — *(screaming)* Make them stop it! *(Both halt. They are in the middle of the room. AMALIA notices his torn clothes.)* Are you hurt? *(She moves to touch him, but his look stops her.)* What are they shouting for? Why doesn't Jones make them stop?
AUGUSTUS	I reckon he can't, Missy. The dead don't make good overseers. *(She stares at him uncomprehendingly.)* Your slaves are revolting, understand?

AMALIA	My slaves? My slaves?
	(runs to the window)
	Make them stop! Augustus, stop them! They'll listen to you!
AUGUSTUS	*(In one bound he has reached the window and grabs her.)*
	Tell me — who was my mother?
AMALIA	Stop them and you'll see — everything will be different! I'll put you in Jones' position. A black overseer. Imagine, you'll be in charge! Prove you are more than a slave and I'll set you free!
AUGUSTUS	Answer me! I've been to your husband. He told me! He confessed!
AMALIA	*(aware of danger on all sides, seeking escape)*
	Confessed? He doesn't know a thing. I am in charge here.
AUGUSTUS	He said he was my father.

AMALIA	Louis, your father?
AUGUSTUS	Ah, Missy, you can't fool me no more. Remember the sewing basket? Lined with blue satin, trimmed with red rosettes?
AMALIA	Rosettes?
AUGUSTUS	The dog didn't have the nerve to kill his own baby outright, so he put a set of spurs in the basket. You know the kind of scars spurs leave, Missy. Like crowns, or exploding suns...
AMALIA	My God!
AUGUSTUS	The woman who patched me up never told me who had brought me. But she kept that basket as a reminder.
AMALIA	(in shock) No...
AUGUSTUS	(shakes her) He said you know who my mother is. Tell me! Tell me! (slaps her) Come on, bitch — who is my mother?

AMALIA   *(wrenching free, her voice trembling with hor-*
ror, toneless and shrill at the same time)

So you want to know, do you?
You want to know your mother?
I have one more story for you —
and when I have finished
you will wish
you had never set your man's foot
on this plantation.
You will wish
you had not stroked my hair
or touched my breasts or
lain with me in that bed.
You will wish
you had no eyes to see
or ears to hear
or mouth to kiss.
You will wish
you had never been born.

AUGUSTUS   Out with it!

AMALIA   I was the one
who put you in that basket.
Yes, I was the one
who sold you — but
it's not like you think.
I wanted to save you.
Save you!
I didn't know about the spurs.
You were so tiny...

(breaks into laughter)

AMALIA (con't.)	My God! My lover then stood as tall as you.
AUGUSTUS ·	Your lover...
AMALIA	Haven't you figured it out yet? Yes, Louis did take to slave girls; ask any of them. Diana has his eyes. But you —
AUGUSTUS	Diana my sister?
AMALIA	— you are not his son! Hector knew; that's why he went to the swamp. And I never touched him again. *(AUGUSTUS looks slowly, desperately at her.)* Now do you understand? I — am — your — mother! *(bursts into wild laughter)* Your mother! *(begins to reel through the room, laughing incessantly)* Your mother!
AUGUSTUS	NO!

(falls to his knees, wild-eyed)

The snakes. So many snakes.

(in a little voice)

The sun and the moon at once.
And the stars.
Don't forget the stars.

PHEBE   *(runs in)*

Augustus! Augustus, they're coming!

(sees AMALIA, hesitates)

They're coming to see if you did
what you were told.
Oh, Augustus, you supposed to kill her!
You've got to run!

AUGUSTUS   Don't cry, girl.
I'll be alright.

PHEBE   *(in tears)*

They'll kill you, Augustus.
Run!

(With a choked cry, AMALIA dashes toward the door. Still on his knees, AUGUSTUS reaches out to stop her.)

AUGUSTUS   Stay!

(*AUGUSTUS clutches AMALIA'S knees; she stares down at him, tenderly pulling his head against her. NED and BENJAMIN rush in, pistols drawn.*)

NED

Bloody traitor!

(*shoots; AMALIA falls*)

AUGUSTUS

Mother...

(*BENJAMIN shoots; AUGUSTUS sinks on top of AMALIA's body*)

PHEBE

Augustus!

(*She kneels beside him. NED and BENJAMIN turn on their heels and leave. The revolting slaves pour in, brandishing sticks and torches.*)

SLAVES

We're free! We're free!

(*SCYLLA is the last to enter. As PHEBE sobs, SCYLLA takes in the scene, staring at the bodies as she slowly straightens up to her full height. Blackout.*)

THE AUTHOR

Rita Dove, U.S. Poet Laureate and Commonwealth Professor of English at the University of Virginia, was born in Akron, Ohio in 1952. She has published five books of poetry, among them *Thomas and Beulah*, which was awarded the Pulitzer Prize. She is also the author of a novel, *Through the Ivory Gate*, as well as a collection of short stories. *The Darker Face of the Earth* is her first full-length play.

Ms. Dove's honors include Fulbright and Guggenheim Fellowships and grants from the National Endowment for the Arts, the National Endowment for the Humanities and the Mellon Foundation. She was chosen by Robert Penn Warren for the Academy of American Poets' Lavan Award, has received a General Electric Foundation award, several honorary doctorates and the Literary Lion citation from the New York Public Library. In 1993 Ms. Dove was appointed Poet Laureate by the Librarian of Congress, received the NAACP Award, and *Glamour* magazine named her as one of the ten "Women of the Year."

THE ILLUSTRATOR

Mark Woolley is an Oregon artist whose work has been published in *The Rockford Review, Zeitgeist, Through the Cracks, sub-TERRAIN, Bohemian Chronicle*, and other magazines. A recipient of a Fulbright fellowship for study in Japan, he opened the Acanthus Gallery in Portland and currently works in the non-profit sector. He has received recognition by the National Trust for Historic Preservation for covered bridge preservation in the Willamette Valley, and has been the Board President for *Sisters of the Road Cafe*, a non-profit dining facility offering low-cost meals and job training to residents of Portland's Old Town.

THE PRESS

Story Line Press, founded in 1985, is an independent, non-profit literary press dedicated to the art and vitality of story.

Based on a farm outside Brownsville, Oregon, Story Line Press fulfills its mission by publishing poetry, novels, short stories, verse plays, creative non-fiction, memoirs, translations, criticism, and essays. For more information about SLP titles please write: Story Line Press / Three Oaks Farm / Brownsville, OR 97327-9718.

KEEPING ALIVE THE STORIES OF OUR TIME.

The publication of
The Darker Face of the Earth
marks the tenth anniversary of Story Line Press.
The edition consists of 4,000 unsigned copies in wrappers;
250 numbered copies, hardbound and signed by the
author; and 26 copies lettered A–Z,
hardbound, and signed by the
author and illustrator.